# 1 MONTH OF
# FREE
# READING

at

## www.ForgottenBooks.com

By purchasing this book you are eligible for one month membership to ForgottenBooks.com, giving you unlimited access to our entire collection of over 1,000,000 titles via our web site and mobile apps.

To claim your free month visit:

www.forgottenbooks.com/free902016

ISBN 978-0-265-86893-5
PIBN 10902016

# hive Document

ntent reflects current scientific knowledge,
es.

IF YOU WANT THE LARGEST, BEST ROOTED, PUREST PLANTS
HERE IS THE PLACE TO GET THEM.

# Farmer's Catalogue

*Berry*
*Fruit*
*Plants*
*Fruit Growers'*
*Supplies, etc.*
*1899...*

## L. J. FARMER,
### FRUIT - GROWER - AND - NURSERYMAN
### PULASKI, N. Y., U. S. A.

HIGHEST AWARD ON STRAWBERRIES AT WORLD'S FAIR
CHICAGO, 1893.

DEMOCRAT PRINT, PULASKI, N. Y.

# FARMER'S FRUIT FARMER

The new paper devoted to the interests of fruit growers in general is edited by L. J. Farmer and published by The Farmer Publishing Co., at Pulaski, N. Y.

## Special Offers to Our Patrons.

We make these special liberal offers in order to induce every one of our patrons to subscribe for our new paper. We want your name on our subscription list and hence these very liberal offers. We would like to send this paper free to all of you, but the Postoffice authorities would not permit it even if we could afford it. It costs us a lot of money to get out this paper and we could not afford to send it free. If you don't want to miss every number, subscribe at once.

Every person ordering plants, etc., from th s catalogue to the amount of $1.00 or more will be entitled to a years subscription to this paper.

**$1.75 FOR $1.00.**

Six dozen Strawberry plants, listed at 25c per dozen, your choice, and Farmer's Fruit Farmer, all postpaid. Special price $1.00.

**$1.85 FOR $1.00.**

Four dozen Raspberries—your choice of varieties listed at 35c per dozen—and Farmer's Fruit Farmer, all postpaid for $1.

**$1.90 FOR $1.00.**

Three dozen Blackberries, listed at 50c per dozen—your choice of varieties—and Farmer's Fruit Farmer, postpaid for $1.

**$2.55 FOR $1.75.**

Grapes—One each of the 12 varieties listed elsewhere and Farmer's Fruit Farmer. Special price postpaid $1.75

**$1.80 FOR $1.00.**

Two Cumberland (30c), 2 Rathbun (25c) 2 Red Cross (20c), 2 Red Jacket (40c), 2 Iceberg (40c), and Farmer's Fruit Farmer. Special price $1 postpaid.

## Read the Following from Our Subscribers.

HANNIBAL, N. Y. Jan. 28th, 1898.

L. J. FARMER—Dear Sir:—Inclosed you will find 15 cents (accor ing to offer No. 2) in your valuable paper received to day) and ten names of fruit growers. Send the paper and 10 plants of the Ea liest strawberry. I will endeavor to get five others to subscribe so I can get the Cam bell Early grape vine. Your p per is needed in this part of N. Y. state. I had rather buy all my plants of you because you are norto nt me. The strawberry plants I received of you last cpring did very well. Yours fraternally, M. A. DuMass.

NORTH ADAMS, Mass., Jan. 30th, 1899.

Many thanks for the sample copy of Farmer's Fruit Farmer which I received a few days ago. It hits my idea of horticultural journal right on the head. I enclose 25c in stamps for a year's subscription. Send six plants of Seaford strawberry. G. W. DALRYMPLE.

FITCHBURG Mass., Jan. 30th, 1899.

Inclosed please find 25c for one years subscription to Farmer's Fruit Farmer. Hoping the paper will continue as good as sample copy. You may send me 6 Ridgway strawberry plants April 15th. A. A. MARSHALL.

BELLOWS FALLS, Vt., Jan 30th, 1899.

I send you 50 cents for two subscriptions. Your paper should be in the hands of every fruit grower. A. A. HALLADAY.

PRIZE OF $5.00 IN GOLD TO CHILDREN.—All who have competed, must send in second letter before April 1st, 1899, when awards will be made.

TO HELP PAY EXPRESS CHARGES.—We will be liberal and put in extras to help pay express charges when patrons live at a distance.

HOW TO SEND COINS BY MAIL.—Send us 3 cents in stamps. We return you 1 cent wrapped safely, showing you how to send coin by mail without using mucilage, coin books, etc., just the sheet of paper your letter is written upon. Worth dollars to you. L. J. FARMER, Pulaski, N. Y.

# To Our Patrons:

ONCE again we come to you with our annual catalogue for the fruit grower. We hope it will lead the way to further orders from you and our better acquaintance. It was just 16 years ago that the writer, a poor boy without funds, borrowed $25 from an older sister to send to E. P. Roe's nurseries for his first strawberry plants to set an acre. Since then we have sent plants to thousands of different people in all parts of the country, starting them into a new and profitable business. This fact is a source of great satisfaction to ourselves. Our catalogue is now mailed annually to over 12,000 different addresses in all parts of America, and we have many friends in different parts of the country who swear by Farmer's plants. To old customers we wish to say that we will continue to serve them faithfully, and to new ones we crave the privilege of receiving and filling your orders. We guarantee the rest.

THE BEST PLANTS THAT GROW are raised on soil that produces the best fruit. Drifting sand that would blow away, were it not for the New York City horse manure, or to use a favorite expression "the marl and mortgages put upon it" is not the ideal place for growing strawberry plants. Might as well say that an animal raised as a scrub the early part of its existence would attain maximum excellence equally as well as if fed rightly from the start. The best trees are grown where those fruits do the best. It was demonstrated at the World's Fair that Oswego County strawberries lead the world. Our diploma and medal proves this. It is shown each year in the large city markets that Oswego berries are the best. Can good berries grow from poor plants? The best plants are produced on strong well drained soil, clay loams, gravelly loams and the like. If earth clings to the roots when digging, all the better for the plants and the planter.

> The man or woman who sets plants this season will be well paid for the effort. Fruits will sell well in 1900. The country is entering upon a period of prosperity as a result of several factors that have been at work. Will you be one of those who have confidence. Fruits have sold low as other crops the past year. Farmers who grow them merely as a make shift will drop the business, the effect will be to make them scarce and higher for the next few years.

## FREEDOM FROM SAN JOSE SCALE AND INSECTS.

There has never been any San Jose Scale discovered in Oswego County, N. Y. The root louse that troubles strawberry plants in so many sections has never been seen in Oswego county, to my knowledge. These are important considerations that the intelligent fruit grower will do well to heed when buying plants.

## COMPETITION WITH CHEAP JOHNNIES.

We cannot compete with men who sell plants for less than they can be produced in our section. We know that when strawberry and other plants are bred for plants only, as many nurserymen advertise, they will mat the ground on loose, sandy soil, as thickly as hair on a dog's back. and can be sold at a profit even at the low prices one often sees advertised. On our strong, loamy soils the plants grow large and not so closely together, and cannot be sold below $3 per 1,000 at a profit. These small, inferior plants are weak and puny when planted, and instead of sending out runners and making new plants the first year, they devote their energies to getting a size on themselves. Our plants are large on the start, they begin to run right off, and by fall cover the surface with plants. They are like a well wintered milch cow—they get there right along.

### ADVICE AND TERMS---Please Read Carefully Before Ordering.

PRICES in this catalogue abrogate all previous quotations.

PAYMENTS.—Invariably in advance. This is the ordinary rule, and it is a good one. We have not the time to inquire about the reliability of patrons in distant parts of the country.

HOW TO SEND MONEY—Small amounts may be sent in bills and stamps. Amounts over $2.00, better be sent by postoffice order, registered letter, express order or draft on New York.

WHEN TO ORDER—We receive and book orders at any time. The earlier you order, the surer you are of getting just what you want. We reserve the right to substitute a variety equally as good if out of any one kind, *unless we are otherwise instructed.*

HOW FAR CAN WE SHIP?—We can ship any distance. Have sent plants to Bermuda, England and the farthest extremes of Canada and Mexico. We make a specialty of sending plants long distances by mail and express. If you live 5,000 miles away, the postage on a package of plants will be no more than if you lived but a few miles from us.

LOW FREIGHT AND EXPRESS RATES— We can secure the lowest freight rates, and the express companies give us a discount of 20 per cent. on all plants sent over their lines.

> This catalogue is sent to you free, hoping that you will favor us with an order. There are a few people who have been receiving our catalogue for some time that have not favored us with an order. These names will not receive catalogues next year unless we hear from them this year either with an order or request to continue their names on our mailing list.

AN IMPORTANT ITEM—Please to remember that in dealing with us, our telegraph, telephone, express, postoffice, bank, etc., are all located at Pulaski.

Yours for fruits,
L. J. FARMER, Pulaski, N.Y.

# STRAWBERRIES.

PERFECT BLOSSOM.

Strawberries do well on any soil, provided it is well drained and fertilized. Grow two or three crops of corn and potatoes previous to setting the strawberry plants. Sandy soils produce early fruits, and clay later. Mulching with straw tends to retard the time of ripening and prevents drying up during a drouth.

Set in straight rows, 3 to 5 feet apart, with plants 1 foot apart in the rows, keep clean of weeds and cut off blossom the first year. Trim off the first 4 or 5 runners and afterwards layer runners at regular intervals about the parent plants. Allow only 4 or 5 runners to root, cut off all others. Scatter ashes or commercial fertilizers around plants and hoe in. Cover plants with straw Dec. 1st and remove in spring, placing between the rows.

Varieties marked "per" will bear alone. Those marked "imp" are imperfect in flower and require those marked "per" to be planted near by them in order to produce a crop. Plants in dozen lots are sent postpaid; add 20c per 100 if wanted by mail, otherwise we will forward by express.

IMPERFECT BLOOM

SAMPLE (imp.) The sample is a new variety originated near Boston, Mass., and was introduced last spring at the enormous price of $5 per dozen; $25 per 100. We purchased 150 plants, sending our check to the amount of $37.50 for the same, besides the express charges. This is the most money we ever paid for so few plants, but in view of what others say in regard to this berry, we are not sorry, however, that we made the venture. We have now over 5,000 plants of our own growing for sale, and will set largely for our own fruiting. We raised over fifty plants from each plant set the past spring and a boy who works for us succeeded in growing over a hundred plants from a single plant, set quite late in the season.

The Sample is a very large, free grow-ing plant. It blooms freely and has all the ear marks of a business berry. It is quite like the Sharpless in appearance of plants.

The Rural New Yorker says: "Sample. The flower is imperfect. The berries are medium to large, regular, heart shaped, crimson, fairly firm and of mild quality. Mr. Pratt claims that 'it is the best berry ever sent out.' We are not at present quite prepared to dispute his claim. The vines are vigorous and very productive. The berries are not only often of the largest size, but are of per-fect shape, and uniformly so. There are

A WELL GROWN STRAWBERRY PLANT.

Note the proportions. The roots are immense, the leaves healthy, the crown large. It is a win-ner. Strawberry plants that are large like this bear transportation and handling better than small weak inferior plants. Our plants grow like this.

no white tips. Considering their size, the berries are firm. Though the peduncles are strong, there are so many berries upon them they lay upon the ground. June 17th was the height of its season. They continued a perfect shape, there being not an irregular berry upon any one of the plants. June 20th still in heavy bearing."

This is what the introducer claimed: "This new berry originated with J. D. Gowing, about five miles from my grounds. Large size and fine quality, quite firm, continues a long time in fruit. The berries are large to the last. For the marketman it is the best-strawberry ever grown. I have nothing in my grounds that will begin to fruit like it. It will yield as many berries as the Haverland and will average as large as Bubach. Colors all over at once. A berry that will do that, is the best one found yet. There is no weak spot in it. Foliage perfect, fruit perfect. Needs no petting."

We are sure it will pay every one to purchase some plants of the Sample strawberry. We consider our stock of them a small gold mine. Price, dozen $1.00; 100, $3.00.

EXCELSIOR (per.) Introduced last spring at $2 per dozen. Originated in Arkansas by the originator of Bismark, West Lawn and VanDeman, and described by him as follows: "The Excelsior is a seedling of the Wilson, grown in a plat with Hoffman. It is a few days earlier than Michel's Early. Larger, higher colored, firmer and immensely more productive. Continues blooming and bearing as long as strawberries last, or until the plants begin to run. It is as strong a plant maker as the Michel. I know this will succeed north and south and fill a long felt want."

With us the plants are great runners and entirely healthy. Doz. 40c; 100, $1.50.

NICK OHMER (per.) Not fruited here. Introduced last spring at $2 per dozen. The introducer speaks as follows: "The Nick Ohmer was originated by John F. Beaver, who is conceded to be the most successful amateur strawberry grower in Ohio. He named it for his friend, N. Ohmer, who has been president of the Montgomery Horticultural Society for more than twenty years, and is ex-president of our State Horticultural Society. Mr. Beaver has fruited nearly all the leading varieties ever introduced in this country, and some from Europe, and when he says that the Nick Ohmer leads any variety he has ever grown, it means

a great deal. It has grown here for three years, and I do not remember having seen any rust on it, but of course every variety will rust under certain conditions. I have sent it to a number on trial and have yet to hear the first unfavorable report. I have no other expectation than that it will become one of the leading varieties, and if restricted to a single one it would be my choice."

We do not want to give this berry a black eye, before we have seen it in fruit, yet we cannot help expressing our fears that it will be a berry for only the best cultivators. 50c per doz,

JERRY RUSK.   Doz. 50c; 100, $2.

DARLING (New).   Per dozen 60c; 100, $2.50.

THE BIG BERRY (New).   Dozen $1.00.

*FARMER'S COLLECTION OF BEST VARIETIES OF WELL-TRIED STRAWBERRIES.*

CARRIE (Imp.) W. J. Green, of Ohio Experiment Station, speaks as follows: "Of the new varieties of strawberries about to be introduced. none pleases me better than Carrie. It resembles the Haverland, but is an improvement upon that variety in size, color and firmness, and it seems equal to it in productiveness." We fruited the Carrie at Maplewood this year. It is just about like Haverland in fruit, except that the fruit is very firm. The plants are very heavy deep rooters and enormously productive. We think this berry will ship long distances by express safely. It ripens very late and lasts a long time. Dozen, 25c; 100, $1.00; 1000, $8.00.

SEAFORD (Imp.) This variety was introduced from Delaware two years ago at $10 per 100. We fruited it here last season and think well of it as a large, productive, firm berry for shipping. It is deep red in color and the color runs right to the core. The plants are enormous runners, making large plants. Very productive and the fruit stalks hold the berries well up from the ground. The introducer describes it as follows: "We state with all sincerity, that, judging from past experience, it is superior to Bubach in many respects, and fully equal in all others, and all intelligent growers have regarded Bubach as being nearer perfection than any other strawberry cultivated here. To be sure it has its defects, and so they all have, but in Seaford we believe we have a berry fully equal to Bubach in size, far more productive, firm enough to meet all requirements, color deep,glossy red, and quality fit for a king. The plant is as large as

in form, attractive in appearance, of good quality and firm enough to stand shipment well. A variety of much prominence."

It has been a long time since we fruited a berry that pleased us so much as did Ridgway, the past season. The plants are healthy rugged growers covering the surface with strong plants that cling to the earth with the persistency of asparagus plants. The berries are large round

Bubach, and a much more vigorous grower, blossom imperfect, while it ripens its crop much faster and several days earlier and therefore commands bigger prices." Dozen 25c; 100, 50c; 1000, $3.50.

L. R. Taft, of Michigan Agricultural Experiment Station, speaks of Seaford as follows:—"The berries are very large, long, broad conical in form, color a dark, rich crimson. The quality is very high and the berry is quite firm."

RIDGWAY (per.) L. R. Taft speaks of it as follows:—"Perfect flower. Plants of excellent growth and a good foliage. Fruit large, short, round conical in form and a bright crimson color. The plants are productive and the fruits very even

shaped like the old Windsor Chief. Color rich scarlet, glossy and firm. We shipped them to Boston and they sold 4c per qt. above Bubach. It ripens mid-season and continues late in bearing. A business berry. Doz. 25c; 1000 60c; 1000 $3 50.

RUBY (per.) A rapid runner and vigorous grower here, but has not fruited yet. Rev. E. B. Stevenson, of Ontario, speaks of it as follows:—"A grand plant, fine grower, fruit large and fine and a good lot of it. The fruit is as large as Bubach, more regular in shape, darker in color, and flesh red all through; shape round, conical, a really good one, and will, I think, take a place as a standard." Dozen 25c; 100, $1.

STAR (per.) Origin Ohio. Plants large light colored and very much resemble Sharpless. Berries very large and of the Sharpless type. Very glossy and high flavored. Parties who like the Sharpless will find Star a great improvement, as it is large and very much more productive. We have a fine stock of plants. Dozen 25c; 100 $1.00.

BARTON (imp). One of the most vigorous growers, largest and most productive berries on the place. It is by no means a new berry, but it is so valuable that we have discarded a score of others in order to grow it largely. We have now the largest stock of this of any variety we grow. The plants are healthy, of the Haverland type, but better runners and more productive. The berries are bright colored, very large elongated and attractive in the baskets, bringing the best prices. No one will miss it if they plant Barton's Eclipse. Dozen 25c; 100 50c; 1000, $3 50.

CLYDE (per.) This variety attracted more attention than any other berry on our grounds, the past season. It is the largest, very early berry and it continues large to the close of the season. The fruits begin to ripen about with Beeder Wood. It is roundish in form and the color is light scarlet The berries are not firm, closely resembling Bubach in this as well as in average size. The plants some times lack enough leaves to properly cover the fruit. Give it plenty of fertilizers and pick when not too ripe and the Clyde will please most everybody. Dozen 25c; 100, 60c; 1000, $3.50.

PARKER EARLE (per.) This well tried variety is still our main standby for a late market fruit. The plants are strong bushy runners, do not make plants rapidly and hence will always command better prices than varieties of the Crescent type. The berries are long, with blunt ends, fair color and firm enough to ship nicely. Its hull recurves and hence the variety is a great favorite with the women folks because a basket of the variety can be hulled so readily. Dozen 25c; 100, 60c; 1000, $4.00.

WILSON (per.) The old favorite for canning. Firm and a good shipper. We have a large stock of extra selected plants which we believe to be the best strain in existence. Dozen 25c; 100,60c; 1000, $3.50.

SPLENDID (per.) The plants of Splendid are perfect growers, entirely healthy, presenting a beautiful appearance glistening in the sun. Berries are large, round and of rich dark color. Enor-

mously productive and one of the best where lots of berries are wanted. Dozen 25c; 100, 50c; 1000, $3.00.

LADY RUSK (imp.) Very similar to the above, perhaps better colored and a trifle firmer. We plant them together for best results. Dozen 25c; 100, 50c; 1000, $3 00.

GLEN MARY (per.) The largest and prettiest plant that we have ever grown. The berries are produced in great abundance, but are rather soft and irregular in shape. It is one of the best where only quantity is wanted, irrespective of appearance, shape or firmness. We have a fine stock. Dozen 25c; 100, 60c; 1000, $3.50.

MARGARET (per.) The introducer describes it as follows:—"The Margaret is large and healthy, and so vigorous in growth that it will mature its last berries and continue green and luxuriant while an abundance of strong runners are produced. The foliage is dark green and so clean and healthy looking that it is a pleasure to work among the plants. The blossom is perfect and one of the strongest ever seen. It commences to ripen soon after early varieties and bears

***

We are located the farthest north of any nursery in the east. Our season is later by several weeks than sections 50 miles south of us, also several weeks later than points on the same latitude farther west. We cannot ship plants quite as early in spring as some, but our plants are dormant when received and do much better, even though your season be well advanced, than plants that are in full bloom and have berries on, as must be the case when ordered from southern nurseries. We ship plants in the month of June and patrons have good success with them. We advise earlier planting, however.

***

until nearly all others are gone. With a good chance, the berries are all of a large size. The plant, with its habit of growth and productiveness, is faultless. The fruit is dark, glossy red, and the berries are not inclined to have white tips. The large, green calyx adds to its beauty. The flesh is firmer than most very large berries, and of excellent flavor. For health, vigorous growth, productiveness, size, beauty and quality, the Margaret is a remarkable variety. "The Margaret was at its best here last summer. We had bushels from ordinary matted rows that contained just about 20 berries to the quart. It continues in bearing over a month, and produced nice berries to the last." Crawford. Dozen 25c; 100, 50c; 1000, $3.50.

**COMPARATIVE SIZES OF VARIETIES.**
1, Saunders; 2, Leader; 3, Lady Rusk; 4) Manchester; 5, Warfield; 6, Van Deman; 7, Jessie; 8, Edgar Queen; 9, Parker Ear e; 10, Bubach; 11, Splendid; 12, Wilson; 13, Beverly; 14, Ignotum; 15, Windsor Chief.

PATRICK (per.) Originator's description. "Most of the extra early berries come from the south, and have not proven especially profitable when grown at the north. Here is a northern berry that promises to be for this section what Michel's Early is for the south. The plant is splendid in growth and foliage and wonderfully vigorous, making runners as freely as Brandywine. The berry is of medium size, about the shape and color of Haverland, of an average quality and firm, with a glossy surface well protected by prominent seeds. It is more productive than Beeder Wood with me, and four or five times as profitable as Michel or VanDeman. "We have not fruited it here, but have a large stock of fine plants. Dozen 25c; 100, 50c; 1000, $3.50.

ENORMOUS AND EDGAR QUEEN (imp.) Some people claim these varieties are distinct. I am quite sure however that they are very similar. The berries are the largest size and bring best money in market. Dozen 25c; 1000, 75c.

ATLANTIC (per.) A berry of the Wilson type. Plants strong sturdy growers. Berries long and very firm. Color rich dark scarlet. Its beautiful, glossy color,

firmness and good size, combined with its season of ripening which is quite late make it one of the profitable varieties in sections where good culture is given. Atlantics from this county lead the markets in getting best prices, often selling for 25 and 35c per quart. Dozen 25c; 100, 60; 1000, $4.00.

HALLS FAVORITE (imp.) A berry very similar to Lady Rush and Splendid in growth of plant and productiveness. Size and shape of the berry about the same. Dozen 25c; 100, 50c; 1000, $3.00.

EARLIEST (per.) This is an extra early berry of the Michels class. It is one of the most healthy, vigorous growers, covering the surface with plants if unrestricted. The berries are medium in size and produced in abundance. It is very fine quality and this quality is never affected by changes in the weather, it is always sweet and nice. Does well in the same bed from year to year. Not a fancy berry for market, but a real good one for home use and for those who appreciate fine flavor. Dozen 25c; 100, 50; 1000, $3.50.

OSWEGO COUNTY QUEEN (per.) A new large irregular shaped berry produced in this section. Berries very large and late. Dozen 25c; 100, $1.00.

WILLIAM BELT. Enormously productive and of the largest size. Plants are some times affected with blight. Dozen 20c; 100, 60c; 1000, $3.50.

BRANDYWINE, CRESCENT, EUREKA, BISEL, OCEAN CITY. Doz. 25c; 100, 50c; 1,000 $3.50

MAXIMUS (per.) New. Dozen 50c; 100, $2.00.

ECHO (per.) New. Dozen 50c; 100, $2.00.

DOLE (per.) New. Dozen $1.00; 100 $6.00.

JOHNSON'S EARLY (per.) New. Dozen 50c; 100, $2.00.

NOTE—The above plants are all of our own growing. We can supply any new variety as cheaply as the introducer. Write us for prices on anything you need. We guarantee satisfaction.

# RASPBERRIES.

The raspberry delights in a well drained, rather loose soil, and will not do well on low wet soils, without drainage. The red varieties should be set in rows six feet apart and one foot apart in the row, when you have plenty of plants, and three feet apart in the row when the plants are scarce. Thus it takes either 2500 or 7000 plants to the acre, depending on the distance apart they are set. We set them close because we have

CUMBERLAND RASPBERRY.

plenty of plants, and thus get a continuous fruiting row quicker than we would to set farther apart. Set black caps in rows seven feet apart and have the plants from one to three feet apart in the row. Thus, it will take of these; 2000 or 6000 plants. Prepare the land thoroughly and plow furrows one foot deep where the rows are to be, setting the plants in a furrow, in a straight line, so that in cultivating you can get up close to them. A hill of beans, potatoes or some other vegetable may be planted between the plants in the row, and also a row of these crops between the rows of raspberries the first year. Give clean culture and pinch back the canes when one foot high, which causes the plant to branch and grow stocky like a tree. The second year, mulch with straw around the bushes and cultivate the middles to keep down weeds, and the ground moist. Pinch the new growing canes back when two feet high, this and succeeding years. and cut the laterals back in early spring, before fruiting. This rigid pruning makes the fruit larger. Remove dead canes after fruiting and maintain level culture. About 200 to 500 plants, made up of the several varieties, should be set for an ordinary family. These will supply fresh fruit for the table and enough to can. Add 5 cents per dozen, 50 cents per hundred, if ordered by mail.

NOTE—Our stock of raspberries is very large and fine, and we won't be undersold by any concern handling the same grade of plants, but if parties wish a large lot of smaller plants, we can quote very much lower prices. These small plants have very nice roots, but the tops are small.

QUEEN OF THE MARKET (Cuthbert) The standard red raspberry. Ripens midseason and continues very late. Fruit large and of the finest flavor, selling for the best prices. Dozen 35c: 100, $1; 1000, $5.00.

GOLDEN QUEEN An albino of the above sort. Enormously productive and of the finest flavor. Dozen 35c; 100, $1.00; 1000, $6.00.

COLUMBIAN RASPBERRY.

COLUMBIAN. Enormously productive. Canes grow tall like trees. Berries purple and good for canning. No one raspberry is its superior for home use. Dozen 50c; 100, $1.50; 1000, $12.00.

MARLBORO. The best early red raspberry, very similar to Cuthbert in appearance but firmer and not quite so high quality. Dozen 35c, 100, $1.00; 1000. $7.00.

ROYAL CHURCH. Dozen 35c: 100, $1.

PHENIX. Dozen 35c; 100, $1.00. LOUDON. The best late raspberry for market. Not so good in flavor as Cuthbert but firmer, larger and more hardy. The canes are stocky and self-supporting. The berries are beautiful. Dozen 35c; 100, $1.50; 1000, $12.00.

MILLER. Dozen 35c; 100, 75c; 1000, $5.00.

SCHAFFER. Dozen 50c; 100, $1.00; 1000; $8.00.

WORTHY. New. Twenty-five cents each; dozen $2.00.

HILBORN. This is the best blackcap we have ever grown at Maplewood Fruit Farm. It is early, large and very productive. We advertised in the local papers for pickers, and hundered of people came from the surrounding towns to pick berries on shares. We gave them every fourth quart. Everybody went home delighted and with their pails full. People will pick on shares when they will not by the quart. Dozen 35c, 100, $100; 1000, $8.00.

CUMBERLAND—This new raspberry originated in Pennsylvania and is supposed to be a seedling of the Gregg with a dash of blackberry blood in it. It is claimed by its friends to be the largest blackcap grown,running nearly one inch in diameter. The Rural New Yorker speaks of it in the highest terms. B. F. Foster,a large grower of Wayne county, writes as follows: "I had five acres of it in fruiting the past summer and am delighted with it. I had Ohio and several other varieties growing side by side with it and under exactly the same conditions The Cumberland fully doubled the yield of Ohio, and is far ahead of all other varieties on my grounds. The fruit is so large and so abundant upon it that it can be easily picked for a third less than other sorts and it is of such a superior appearance as to command usually a little above the market price of other varieties. I cannot too strongly recommend this new berry." 20c. each, 2 for 30c. Dozen $1.50.

# BLACKBERRIES.

Require the same soil as raspberries. Set in rows eight feet apart, with plants from one to three feet apart in the row. Thus it takes from two to five thousand for an acre. Cultivate and prune like raspberries. Shave off all suckers that spring up between the rows, and keep the plants in narrow, continuous rows. Mulch with straw about the plants during fruiting season to keep the soil moist. Always cultivate blackberries very shallow, so as not to injure the roots. Every broken root sends up an additional sucker to interfere with cultivation. Add 5c per dozen, 50c per hundred, if ordered by mail. Blackberries make a very paying crop when the markets are not overrun with wild ones. It will pay the farmer to have a supply in his garden; 'tis much easier than chasing the woods for wild ones.

NOTE—We have an immense stock of standard varieties and will make low rates to large planters. Write for estimates.

## WHITE BLACKBERRY "ICEBERG."

(Raised by Luther Burbank, the "Wizard of Horticulture.")

The following is Mr. Burbank's own description, and its accuracy will be vouched for by all who know him, as he is commendably conservative in all that he says about his creations. In his desire to mislead no one, he leans rather toward underrating than exaggerating the value of his originations. He says:

"Owing to the somewhat unsatisfactory qualities of White Blackberries so far known, the impression may have been entertained by some that no White Blackberry could be as productive and hardy, with berries as early, abundant, large, handsome and delicious, as the best black ones.

"The well known Lawton is, when ripened, unsurpassed, and very generally known as the most productive market berry. Owing to its fixity of race, it will reproduce itself from seed almost exactly, and its seedings will not be influenced, when raised from seed pollenated by other varieties, but it readily imparts its good qualities when employed as the staminate parent. One of the great grandparents of 'Iceberg' was Lawton. The first generation of seedlings, when crossed with Crystal White, was all black; the second also, though varying much in other respects; but the third produced this wonderful plant, bearing the snowiest white berries ever seen.

"Very little attention was paid to the long rows of cross-bred descendants, until one day this berry was discovered, among its black relatives, with the canes bending in various directions with their load of delicious, snowy berries, which are not only white, but so transparent that the seeds, which are unusually small, may be seen in the berries when ripe.

"Clusters, larger than those of Lawton; berries, as near as could be judged, were at least as large, earlier, sweeter, and more tender and melting throughout, though as firm as Lawton is when ripe." 20c each; dozen $2.00.

RATHBUN. Prof. Bailey writes July 21, 1896—"The Rathbun blackberry is now in full fruit, and we are much pleased with it. It is midway between a blackberry and dewberry in habit, as also in earliness. The berries are exceedingly large, glossy, jet black, and of good quality. I certainly think that there is a future for it." 2 for 25c; dozen $1.25; 100, $6.50.

MERSEREAU. Prof. Bailey, who named this variety, has this to say about it—"A variety resembling Snyder and derived from it. Some four years ago the originator noticed an extra large strong bush among his Snyders and began to pro- pagate from it. He is now gradually changing his whole plantation over to this new variety, it is one of the most promising varieties I know." ? for 30c: dozen $1.50; 100, $8.50.

SNYDER. Best hardy early variety. Dozen 50c; 100, $1.00; 1000 $8.00.

TAYLOR. Best hardy late variety, sweet. Dozen 50c; 100, $1.00; 1000, $8.

AGAWAM, WESTERN TRIUMPH, LUCRETIA KITTATINNY, STONE'S HARDY. Dozen 50c; 100, $1.00.

ERIE, MAXWELL'S EARLY, ELDORADO, ANCIENT BRITON, WACHUSETT THORNLESS, LOVETT. Dozen 50c; 100, $2.00.

# GOOSEBERRIES.

The gooseberry is a fruit that will pay if a market can be secured for it. Comparatively few people are used to it; however a taste can be readily acquired; There is no fruit with us that goes better than canned gooseberries. The American varieties are smaller than the English, but are free from mildew and bear enormous crops if the worms are kept off. The English varieties may be grown by spraying with liver of sulpher or Bordeaux mixture, which will prevent mildew. Watch the gooseberries and currants in early spring and spray with Paris green water as soon as the worms appear. If not attended to in the right time, it takes but a few days for the leaves to be entirely stripped. The berries then ripen prematurely and dry up in the sun.

HOUGHTON. A small, pale red, smooth variety of fine quality. The plants are entirely free from disease and the most productive of any gooseberry in cultivation. This and Downing are the varieties generally grown in our gardens. Two years old, dozen, 40c; 100, $2.0.

DOWNING. Very much larger than Houghton, producing nearly as much bulk of fruit. Color, pale green. The favorite American variety. Dozen, 50c; 100, $2.50.

SMITH. Same price.

PEARL. An American sort claimed to be the most free from disease and the most prolific gooseberry grown. Dozen, $1.00; 100, $7.00.

**NATURAL SIZE**

RED JACKET. Nearly as large as the English varieties, free from mildew and very productive. Color, pale red. We are delighted with it. Twenty cents each; dozen, $1.50; $10 per 100.

We grow our own plants on the best soil. Two acres of this land sowed to wheat last season yielded 96 bushels and enough straw to properly cover three acres of berries.

KEEPSAKE AND INDUSTRY. Valuable English varieties, much grown in this country. Twenty cents each; dozen, $2.00; 100, $10.00.

CHAUTAUQUA. A large variety supposed to be a cross of the American and English types. Not so subject to mildew as the English varieties, Bush stout and vigorous. Berries very large, often over an inch in diameter. Color, pale yellow; very sweet; productive. Twenty-five cents each; dozen, $3.00.

Our gooseberry plants are all two years old. Some three years old.

Add 10c per dozen if sent by mail: 50c per 100 for currants and gooseberries.

# CURRANTS.

Plant on very rich soil, made so by repeated applications of rich barn fertilizers and potash salts applied to the crops that precede currants. It takes 2,904 plants to the acre, set in rows 5x3. Give clean culture and mulch with straw about the bushes during the fruiting season. Cut out old wood after it has borne several crops and replace by allowing new canes to grow from the roots. Keep the plant in upright bush form and do not allow it to become crowded. If you allow weeds and grass to grow around them, currants will be a failure in both quantity and quality of fruit. We spread a shovelful of manure and a quart of ashes about each plant, in November, and have wonderful success with currants and gooseberries.

RED CROSS. (New.) Originated by Jacob Moore, of Rochester, N. Y., and sold to the introducers for $1,250, cash. We have eaten the fruit, and can endorse it. Prof. Maynard, of Hatch experiment station, Massachusetts, says Red Cross, as seen at Rochester, averages larger than Fay's Prolific and is more vigorous. Jacob Moore, the originator, says it is twice as large as Victoria, will yield twice as much as Cherry and is of better quality than any of the older varieties. P. C. Reynolds, the veteran horticulturist of Rochester, says that the Red Cross currant averages larger than Fay or Cherry and is sweeter than most other varieties. He says that the clusters are longer, and that the size of the berries hold out larger to the end of cluster than Fay. Ten cents each; doz. 60c; 100, $4.50; two-years-olds, doz. $1; 100, $7.

POMONA. (New.) A new currant originated in Indiana; claimed to be very large and enormously productive. As a money getter it has a wonderful record at its home. Ten cents each; dozen 75c; two-years-old, dozen, $1.00.

NORTH STAR. (New.) This variety is claimed by its friends to be the hardiest, the best grower, the most prolific bearer, the sweetest and best currant grown. We have fruited it two years, and think well of it. The berries are not so large as Fay, but more productive and sweeter. Ten cents each; dozen 50c; 100, $3.00.

FAY'S PROLIFIC. Our favorite among the well tried varieties for market. Seems to do better on light soil than others. The berries are very large and will bring the best prices in market. We have them almost as big as cherries. Dozen, 50c; 100, $2.50; two-year-olds, dozen, 70c; 100,|$3.50.

WHITE GRAPE. The largest and most productive white currant grown. Flavor, sweet and very fine for the table. Not desirable for the general markets, because people don't seem to take to white fruits. The best table currant. Price same as Fay.

BLACK NAPLES, CHAMPION, CHERRY, LA VERSAILLES, LEE'S, PRINCE ALBERT, RED DUTCH, VICTORIA. Same price as Fay.

# · GRAPES

Grapes do best in a sunny location on the south side of fences, buildings and hillsides where the sun will play over them nearly all day. The soil must be loose and open, and well drained. Every farmer should have 25 to 100 vines for the family use. There is no fruit more health giving. They follow closely after small fruits, and save many a doctor's bill. This innocent fruit has often been made the victim of boards of health and sensationalists, but it has come out of the furnace unscathed. There has yet to be proved that any case of appendicitis was caused by eating grapes, nor has anybody been poisoned by Bordeaux mixture when sprayed on the fruit. The great secret of success in growing grapes lies in knowing how to trim them. Many a vine that is now running wild might be made fruitful by proper trimming. The novice will either trim too much or too little. They require fertilizing much the same as other fruits. Our ideas of growing are as follows: Select one or two year old vines and set them in furrows one foot deep and eight feet apart. Plant the vines ten feet apart in the furrows. Put a little surface soil in the bottom, spread the roots out both ways, so as to run parallel with the rows, and cover with fine, loose soil, filling in the furrow. Keep the soil loose and open, and do not plow deep enough to injure the roots. Practice shallow cultivation. Use plenty of mineral fertilizers, rich in potash. There are various methods of trimming the vine, but probably the following is the most simple and easy: Allow only one cane to grow the first year; rub off all other buds. Build a trellis, using wire or horizontal slats. In the fall of the first year, raise the cane up to the top wire and cut off all cane above the wire. Lay the cane down and cover with some coarse litter to protect it through the winter. In the spring tie the cane to the wire so it will stand upright or perpendicular. Allow two buds to grow into canes at the top; rub off all buds below. These buds are to produce the canes which are to be tied to the upper wire in a horizontal position the next spring. They are cut back to four feet in the fall, and if the climate is severe, all are taken from the wires, laid down and covered for the winter. In the spring the whole vine is put up and tied to the wire. The vine is now in the shape of the letter "T." From all along the horizontal cane tied to the upper wire, the buds produce the canes that bear the fruit. These little canes are all cut back close to the horizontal canes each fall, leaving little spurs with three buds each. From these spurs grow more green canes each year which bear the fruit. By this method there need be no summer tying of the green, growing canes. By the old method we tied the canes to the lower wire and as they grew we tied the green canes which bear the fruit, to the upper wire. There need be no trouble in trimming the grape, if one understands the principle. Many people trim too little, others so severely that they remove all the bearing wood. Grapes are borne on green wood that grows the same season as the fruit, upon wood that grew the year before. So in trimming be sure to leave on some of the last year's growth. If you leave on too much or too little, the results are about the same—you get wood and no fruit. When your canes get old and unfruitful, fertilize more, encourage new canes to grow from the roots to replace the old ones which should be removed.

## CAMPBELL'S EARLY GRAPE.

This new grape was produced by the late Geo. W. Campbell, of Ohio. Another season's experience confirms and strengthens the entire confidence heretofore expressed in this noble variety. It was mistaken in the Buffalo markets this year for Black Hamburg, it was so large and fine looking, selling for twice the price of other varieties of the same season. The following are the especial points of merit in Campbell's early grape:

First. A very strong, vigorous, hardy vine, with thick, healthy, mildew resisting foliage and perfect, self-fertilizing blossoms; always setting its fruit well, and bearing abundantly.

Second. Clusters very large, usually shouldered, compact and handsome, without being unduly crowded.

Third. Berries large, nearly round, often an inch or more in diameter; black with light purple bloom; skin thin but very tenacious, bearing handling and shipping admirably. Flavor rich, sweet, slightly vinous; pure with no foxiness, coarseness or unpleasant acidity from the skin to the center. Flesh rather firm but tender and of equal consistency, parting easily from its few and small seeds. As more than one-third of the

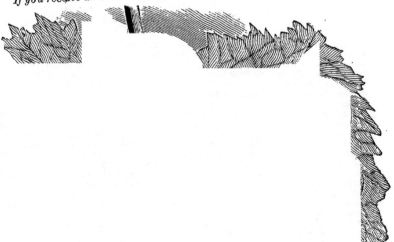

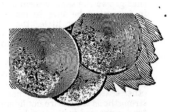

**Campbell's Early Grape**

American people do not and will not swallow grape seeds, we consider this a strong point in favor of Campbell's Early and a matter of trade well worth earnest attention, for as Prof. Lintner, New York State Entomologist, well says "No grape seeds may be safely swallowed."

Fourth. Its season is very early; often showing color late in July, and ripening, according to the season, from the fifteenth to the last of August, at Delaware, Ohio.

Fifth. It has very remarkable keep-ping qualities. Has hung upon the vines in the fall of 1897, sound and perfect, for six weeks or more after ripening, with no tendency to shell off or fall from the stem. A few crates were put in a cool cellar Oct. 5th this year and are now (Dec. 20th) apparently as perfect as when stored and looking as though they may keep in equally good condition until next April. As a good keeper and shipper it is believed to be unequalled by any other American grape.

### BEST HARDY GRAPES--2 years, first-class, postpaid.

|  | EACH | PER 10 |
|---|---|---|
| CAMPBELL'S EARLY—Black, earliest, good grape | $1.00 | $8.00 |
| WORDEN—Black, earlier than Concord | .10 | .60 |
| AGAWAM—Dark red, ripens after Concord | .10 | .60 |
| BRIGHTON—Dark red, one of the best table grapes | .10 | .70 |
| CATAWBA—Late, red, does not succeed everywhere | .10 | .60 |
| CONCORD—Black, medium, king of all grapes | .10 | .60 |
| DELAWARE—Light red, bunches and berries of medium size | .10 | .70 |
| MOORE'S DIAMOND—White, hardy, very popular | .10 | .70 |
| MOORE'S EARLY—Black, two weeks earlier than Concord | .10 | .70 |
| NIAGARA—White. very large, vigorous and productive | .10 | .60 |
| POCKLINGTON—White, very large, showy | .10 | .60 |
| GREEN MOUNTAIN—Best early white grape, sweet | .35 | 3.00 |

One year old vines at three-fourths price of above.

**No.** 380

## State of New York,

# Department of Agriculture

### Certificate of Inspection of Nursery Stock.

This is to certify that the stock of the Nursery of *L. J. Farmer,* of *Pulaski,* County of *Oswego,* State of New York, was duly examined in compliance with the provisions of Chapter 482 of the Laws of 1898, and it was found to be apparently free in all respects from any contagious or infectious plant disease or diseases, or the San Jose scale or other dangerously injurious insect pest or pests.

Dated *December 1, 1898,* Albany, N. Y.,

*C. A. Wieting,*
Commissioner of Agriculture.

# ASPARAGUS.

Any well drained soil will do for asparagus. Mark the rows four to five feet apart and plant the roots in trenches made deep with the plow, about one foot apart. Thus it takes about as many plants to the acre as of strawberries. Cover the plants with loose soil and gradually fill in the trenches as the plants grow. Allow the canes to grow without cutting until the third year. Then in the spring, as soon as eight or ten inches high, cut or break off the tender portion above the ground. Cuttings may be made each year as late in the season as strawberry time. Give clean culture and mow off the canes in winter and burn. Salt the soil about the plants once in a year to keep down the weeds. This vegetable is not only very palatable when cooked as green peas, but is valuable as a medicine for the kidneys. Conover's Colossal. Palmetto and Barr's Mammoth, doz. 25c; 100, $1; 1000, $5, for two year old roots. Columbian, White and Donald's Elmira, doz. 35c; 100, $1.25; 1000, $6. Add 5c per doz., 30c per 100, if by mail.

RHUBARB. Ten cents each; $5 per 100.

HORSERADISH CUTTINGS. Dozen 25c; hundred $1.50.

SAGE. Holt's Mammoth. Dozen, 30c; hundred, $2.

# NOVELTIES.

Not content with the fruits that grow well and produce good crops under ordinary conditions, the nurseryman and fruit grower is ever looking for new types of fruit to experiment with. The results are generally disappointing. Most of the remuneration consists in the novelty of the observations. Not wishing to be behind the lighthouse, we have tried the Wineberry, Mayberry, Strawberry-Raspberry, Rocky Mountain Cherry and Buffalo Berry, etc., etc.

The Japanese Wineberry grows like a raspberry. The canes and leaves are greenish purple when growing and the ripened canes are dark red in color. It is a very vigorous grower and increases from the tip ends. The canes are covered with thorns more prominent than our common raspberries. The fruit is bright, glossy red, rather soft and about the same size as common black caps. It is produced from a burr like a beechnut which opens as the fruit ripens. The plants are very productive. The fruit is not high flavored, rather insipid to most tastes. It makes the best pies of any raspberry, so says the wife of the proprietor of our largest hotel, who took most that we grew the past season. It is fairly good on the table as a novel fresh fruit. Its beautiful color sells it in market. The canes are very tender however and the plant is not adapted for this northern country. They are said to be hardy as far north as New York city. The first winter after the plants are set, they may be covered like strawberries with straw as the canes sprawl out like blackcaps, but after the first winter I cannot suggest an economical means of covering, as the canes are upright. A plant or so could be covered by standing corn stalks and other material around it, but this would be too expensive on a large scale, so the cultivation of the wineberry for market must be confined to warmer localities. The plant, leaves and fruit are beautiful and it would pay one who has never seen them to try it. Ripens with blackberries.

Ten cents each; dozen, 50c; 100, $1.25; 1000, $10.

The Mayberry is said to be a cross of the Cuthbert raspberry and the wild Mayberry of Japan. We have had it for several years, but the canes have always frozen back and winterkilled, so they have borne no fruit. It is a pretty growing plant, rather dwarfish in habit, and the canes are very thorny. This year we have, to winter, a cane about 2½ feet high. This is the longest cane we have ever had. It reproduces itself sparingly from suckers like red raspberries, and of course more readily by root cuttings. Three years old, 25c each; dozen, $2.

The Strawberry-Raspberry is borne on a plant that grows dwarfish like the strawberry plant. Every spring the plant sends up canes about the length of one foot and the berries are borne on the top and branches of this cane. This cane dies down in the fall. The fruit is very like the wineberry in color and size of drupelets. The berry is nearly as large as ordinary strawberries and is borne on a receptacle like blackcaps. The fruit is even more lacking in flavor than the wineberry. I might say that it is worthless, except for show. It is salvy, flimsy and tastes "vinous," if it has any taste at all. The plants bear very sparingly and appear to have all the qualifications of a first-class weed. It increases readily from broken pieces of the roots. We have not increased our original plantation of this fruit. Ripens in August. Ten cents each; dozen, $1; 100, $5.

The Rocky Mountain cherry is a very hardy shrub having the appearance of dwarf willows. The canes are tough, slender and lined with smooth leathery leaves. It grows about three feet high and may be set closely together like currants or gooseberries. The blossoms are very small, not much larger than currant blooms, and the fruit, which is black and the regular size of cherries, is strung on thick the entire length of the cane. It is an enormous bearer and the plants are entirely hardy, but the fruit is rather poor quality and quite susceptible to rot. Of course the rot could be controlled by spraying with Bordeaux. The plant increases from off-shoots and layers and probably from cuttings, although I have not tried this last way. I consider the Rocky Mountain cherry the most promising of all the novelties I have tried. Ripens in August. Twenty-five cents each; dozen, $2.50,

The Buffalo berry is a native of the Rocky mountains like the R. M. cherry and like that fruit is not adapted to the east where better fruits can be grown more readily. It is a shrub, grows upright. Plants I have had 4 or 5 years are now 4 to 6 feet high. There were a few berries produced this year, but they dropped off prematurely or were taken by the birds, early in the season. The berries are red and are said to be very sour till frost comes when they improve by freezing. The shrub makes a very pretty appearance with its silvery leaves. It increases from shoots that spring up

from the roots, very sparingly. Both of these Rocky mountain fruits do better on high dry ground. They do not like the wet. Twenty-five cents each; $2.50 doz.

Of Eleagnus Longipes, Wm. Falconer, the editor of "Gardening," and superintendent of the late Charles A. Dana's Dosoris Gardens, says: "The shrub Eleagnus Longipes is one of my special favorites. I have grown it for years and the longer I know it the better I like it. It is a native of Japan and belongs to the olive family of plants, and is entirely hardy. As a garden shrub it grows to a height of five feet or more, is bushy, broad and thrifty; plants begin to fruit when two or three years old. The leaves are oval, oblong, green above, silvery beneath and last in good condition all summer long and are never disfigured by insect vermin. The flowers are small, silvery yellow and borne in great abundance, and are in full bloom about the 6th to 10th of May. The fruit is oval, five-eighths of an inch long, very fleshy and juicy, bright red and drooping, on slender pedicles on the under side of the twigs and borne in immense profusion. It is ripe about July 4th to 10th. We use the fruit for sauce as one would cranberries, and a delicious sauce it makes, especially for children. Indeed I like it so well that I have planted it in our fruit garden as a standard crop, as one would currants."

Price, 2 years old, 20c; 3 years old. 25c; 4 years old, 30c, postage paid.

The Dwarf Juneberry has not fruited with us, but said to resemble the swamp huckleberry and is a good substitute for that fruit, being of easy culture. The habit is similar to the currant, the bushes attaining the same size, and are literally loaded with fruit in June. The blossoms are large and composed of fine white petals, which, with its bright, glossy, dark green foliage, renders it one of the handsomest ornamental shrubs. Fifteen cents each; dozen $1.

# ROSES.

The rose blooms when strawberries ripen, and I suppose that is one reason why it is my favorite flower. We have lots of them all through the summer, and everybody enjoys them. They may easily be grown out doors if the following varieties are planted. Set the plants in moist, rich soil and prune quite severely every spring. Cover with boards and straw on the approach of cold weather and there need be no failure. Our plants are two years old and not to be compared with small hot house roses, grown in pots. Price 25c each; dozen $2 50.

YELLOW RAMBLER. (See illustration.) This is a new rose of the climbing sort, now introduced for the first time. The growth is very vigorous, often making, in well established plants, ten feet in one season. It is quite hardy, enduring zero weather without protection. It is of the same habits as Crimson Rambler, the flowers being borne in immense clusters. The color is decidedly yellow. The blossoms are of moderate size and are very sweetly scented; it lasts three to four weeks without fading. 30c each.

CRIMSON RAMBLER. This is a very vigorous grower, often making ten feet in one season. It is enormously prolific of blooms, 430 buds and blossoms being counted on one shoot. It is entirely hardy and should be in every door yard, climbing over the porch. Thirty cents each.

AMERICAN BEAUTY. Enormous buds and full flowers. Color, deep, glowing carmine.

COQUETTE DES ALPES. Large, white, always double sometimes faintly tinged with pink; a free bloomer.

EARL OF DUFFERIN. The finest dark red rose; rich, brilliant, velvety, crimson, shaded dark maroon, beautifully formed and highly scented.

GENERAL JACQUEMINOT. Best known and most admired of all crimson roses.

GENERAL WASHINGTON. Brilliant crimson flowers of full, broad form; blooms constantly.

MADAME PLANTIER. The cemetery rose. Flowers medium size, full, sweet, and produced in great numbers. The purest white known in roses. Entirely hardy and blooms very early.

MAGNA CHARTA. Color, a clear, rosy red, beautifully flushed with violet crimson. Flowers extra large and very double. Very fragrant and a profuse bloomer.

MRS. JOHN LAING. Splendid size and full. Color, clear, deep pink; fragrance delightful; blooms first season.

QUEEN OF THE PRAIRIE. A very valuable climbing rose. Pale pink in color and a profuse bearer.

PRINCE CAMILLE DE ROHAN. The darkest and richest of the red black roses.

VICK'S CAPRICE. A striped rose of glossy pink, dashed and flamed with white and carmine.

BALTIMORE BELLE. One of the finest climbing roses. Color white; medium in size and a free bloomer.

PAUL NEYRON. The very largest of all roses. Color, very bright, clear rose, deepening to crimson; fragrant and free bloomer.

The prices of the above hardy perpetual roses is 25c each; $2.50 per dozen. The dozen may be all different kinds if desired. Postage paid.

# CRATES AND BASKETS.

The 36 quart Baker's Patent Berry Crate is the best crate used for shipping strawberries that we have ever seen. It is the crate used exclusively in Oswego county, N. Y., for shipping to Boston, New York, Philadelphia and other markets. We can supply these crates filled with nice clean new baskets at 60c each; 50c each where 10 or more are ordered at one time; extra baskets at $4.00 per 1000; lighter baskets $3.00 per 1000. Send in your order for crates and baskets before the berry season opens. We are sometimes unable to supply crates and baskets late in the season.

RUTLAND CO., Vt., August, 19th, 1898.
Plants rec- ived all right last week, came in fine order, did not heat. Have them all set out and think with the heavy rain we are getting today they will come nicely. M.D. CAMPBELL.

CAYUGA CO., N. Y., June 11th, 1898.
The plants you sent me arrived in good shape. I do not think more than a dozen will die, The Atlantic have the most roots of any berry I have seen. L. V. DEGRAFF.

ROUSES POINT, N. Y June 1st, 1898.
The strawberry plants came to hand, and were perfectly satisfactory, splendid plants in all respects. WM. B. MILLARD.

BROOKLYN, N. Y., Aug. 31st, 1898.
The plants are fine ones and are looking well, J. S. KITTLE.

WATERVLIET, N. Y., May 27, 1898.
Strawberry plants were re-eived in good order and are now doing nicely.
L. D. COLLINS.

EAST BRIDGEWATER, Mass., May 16, 1898.
Package of vines, (grapes) received Friday evening and were satisfactory.
K. E. SHELDON.

FON DU LAC, Wis., May 10. 1898.
Received the basket of Edgar Queen strawberries. They are in fine shape.
JOHN H. SHOULDER.

CORTLAND, N. Y., May 2, 1898.
Strawberry plants are here, No. 4662. They look nice. GEO. W. CLAKK.

RUTLAND, Vt., May 6, 1898.
The plants you expressed to us April 29th reached u. in good condition witho.t delay. They are fine. My husband says they are the nicest lot of plants he ever saw.
Mrs. GEO. FARRINGTON.

MT. HOPE, Ohio. May 10tb, 1898.
I received the plants in good order.
MRS. L. F. ROTTMAN.

NORTH SANBORNTON, N. H., May 2nd, 1898.
Tho plants shipped April 29th arrived in good order and am well pleased with them
H. H. SANBORN.

ST. PAUL, Minn., May 20th, 1898.
I received all my plants yesterday... They were in good con ition and looked very nice.
MRS. ANDREW PETERSON.

WINTHROP, Wash., April 12th, 1898.
I received your bill of black cap raspberries and they were in extra fine shape. I am well pleased with yc ur selection of kinds and will recommend your nursery to my neighbors. Thanking you for prompt shipment, etc.
W. K. HULETT.

BEDFORD. Ind., Ap-il 14th, 1898.
Plants arrived all right and in good condition. R. B. WOODY.

HILLS POINT, Md., March 27th, 1898.
The plants arrived yesterday in nice shape. I thank you for filling my order so promptly.
E. F. BUSICK.

CLARKS SUMMIT, Pa., April 26th, 1898.
Plants were received the 24th, in good order.
WM. ATHERTON.

WEST POINT, Miss., March 26th, 1898.
, The strawberry plants I ordered for you came several d. ys ago. The plants were in good condition. G. L. MAXSON.

CLARKSBURGS, Mo., March 23rd, 1898.
I received the straw berry plants yesterday in good order (! o. 4,500). You will get my orders hereafter. ESTELLE LOWRY.

MILTON, N. Y., March 28th, 1898.
Package of plants received O. K. Thanks.
C. S. NORTHRUP.

CUYAHOGA Falls, O., May 12th, 1898.
Two bask-ts of Margaret rec-ived all right.
M. CRAWFORD.

ENGLEWOOD, N. Y., March 30th. 1898.
Stock arrived all right and in good condition. A.l look especially fine. M. MATTISON.

*From the Junior Republic.*

FREEVILLE, N. Y., May 9th, 1898.
The strawberry plants reached us in good condition and we are very grateful to you for them. We hope you may find an opportunity to visit us in the future. Sincerely,
MRS. W. K. GEORGE.

# The Best and Newest Rural Books.

The following is a brief description of two series of books on the leading topics connected with outdoor or rural life. Each book is the work of a competent specialist, under the editorial supervision of Prof. L. H. Bailey, of the Cornell University, and will be found readable, clear-cut practical and thoroughly up-to-date, treating its topics in a plain but comprehensive way, from the same general standpoint of combining science and practice. These books tend through-out to inform the reader as to principles, so that he may think out his problems for himself.

# THE RURAL SCIENCE SERIES

Includes books which state the underlying principles of agriculture, and their adaptation to modern practical work, in plain language. They are suitable for consultation alike by the amateur or professional tiller of the soil, the scientist or the student. Illustrations of marked beauty are freely used. and the books are clearly printed and well bound. New volumes will be added to the Rural Science Series from time to time.

THE SOIL. Its Nature, re'ations and fundamental principles of management. By F. H King, Professor of Agricu'tural Physics in the University of Wisconsin.

303 PAGES—45 ILLUSTRATIONS—75 CENTS.

A luminous and practical discussion of the soil and its various attributes. As an understanding of the soil in some measure is of vital necessity to s' ccess in even the most limited agricultural opera'ions, the importance of a work like this cannot easily be overestimated. The progressive farmer will be greatly helped by a thoughtful perusal of this book.

THE FERTILITY OF THE SOIL
A summary sketch of the relationship of

farm practice to the maintaining and increasing of the productivity of the soil. By I. P. Roberts, Director of the College of Agriculture. Cornell University. SECOND EDITION—432 PAGES—45 ILLUSTRATIONS $1.25.

This work, written by one who has been termed "the wisest farmer in America," takes up the treatment of the soil from the standpoint of the farmer rather than that of a scientist. It embodies the results of years of careful experimentation and observation along practical lines, and will be found helpful and inspiring to a marked degree.

## THE SPRAYING OF PLANTS

A succinct account of the history, principles and practice of the application of liquids and powders to plants for the purpose of destroying insects and fungi. By E. G. Lodeman, late Instructor in horticulture in the Cornell University.
399 PAGES—92 ILLUSTRATIONS—$1.00.

In these days this subject is conceded to be of great importance to the horticulturist; for it is only by intelligent spraying that many large fruit interests are saved from utter extinction. Professor Lodeman treats the subject both historically and practically, and this authoritative work forms the only complete manual of spraying. The diseases and insects to be combatted are also fully presented.

## THE PRINCIPLES OF FRUIT GROWING.

By L. H. Bailey, Professor of Horticulture in the Cornell University.
520 PAGES—114 ILLUSTRATIONS—$1.25.

There have been manuals and treatises on fruit growing, but this volume is the first consistent presentation of the underlying principles affecting the growth of the various fruits. It is thus unique, and it occupies a field of the greatest importance. It joins science and practice, for it not only discusses the reasons for certain operations, but presents the most approved methods, gathered from the successful fruit growers of America.

## BUSH-FRUITS.

A horticultural monograph of Raspberries, Blackberries, Dewberries, Currants, Gooseberries and other shrub-like fruits. By Fred W. Card, Professor of Horticulture in Rhode Island Agricultural College.
537 PAGES—113 ILLUSTRATIONS—$1.00.

The aim of this book is two-fold—to give all necessary instruction on the cultivation of the bush fruits, and to provide a cyclopedia of reference to varieties, species, insects and diseases. Every variety of the various fruits is fully described, this being the first effort to collect information about varieties of all these fruits since the time of the Downings. In this respect the book will always be a standard authority. The varieties are arranged alphabetically under various natural classes or groups, but a very full index refers instantly to any variety.

## FERTILIZERS.

The source, character and composition of natural, home-made and manufactured fertilizers; and suggestions as to their use for different crops and conditions. By Edward B. Voorhees, Director of the New Jersey experiment station and Professor of Agriculture in Rutgers College.
335 PAGES—$1.00.

This book discusses the difficult question of fertilizers in such plain and untechnical language that those who are wholly unlearned in chemistry can use it. There are no elaborate tables. The book instructs upon the fundamental principles of the use of fertilize s, so that the farmer is able, when he reads it, to determine for himself what his practice shall be. It is not an advocate for commercial fertilizers, but tells simply and directly what the truth is regarding their value. It explains the latest results of experiments to determine what fertilizers are best for given soils and given crops.

---

## THE GARDEN-CRAFT SERIES

Comprises practical hand-books for the gardener or florist, explaining and illustrating in detail the various important methods. They may be called manuals of practice, and though all are written by Professor Bailey, of Cornell University, they include the opinions and methods of specialists in many lines. They are illustrated, bound in flexible cloth, and are convenient for reference on the desk or in the greenhouse or the field.

## THE HORTICULTURIST'S RULE BOOK.

A compendium of useful information for fruit growers, truck gardeners and others. By L. H. Bailey, Professor of Horticulture in the Cornell University.
FOURTH EDITION—312 PAGES—75 CENTS.

A vast mass of information is presented in this handy little reference book, arranged so carefully and indexed so completely that instant reference may be made to any one of the two thousand entries. The things you want to know about horticultural work, the remedy for a plant disease, the way to conquer a troublesome insect enemy—all are concisely set forth. It is a collection of verified and digested facts, in compact form easy of reference and comprehensive in range. Now in its fourth edition, the book has become a standard reference work.

## THE NURSERY BOOK.

A complete guide to the multiplication of plants. By L. H. Bailey, Professor of Horticulture in the Cornell University.
THIRD EDITION—365 PAGES—152 ILLUSTRATIONS $1.00.

The detailed questions of propagation are answered in this admirable volume, which has become the standard work of reference for nurserymen. It is now in its third edition, and has been thoroughly revised and greatly extended. It is intensely practical and fully sets forth the processes of budding, grafting, seed-sowing, etc., as well as many other important items of nursery work. It is simply essential to the seedsman, nurseryman florist or grower of plants in any walk of life. As with all Prof. Bailey's works, there are unusually complete indexes and glossaries, rendering the book most convenient in use.

## PLANT-BREEDING.

Being five lectures upon the amelioration of domestic plants. By L. H. Bailey, Professor of Horticulture in the Cornell University.
293 PAGES—20—ILLUSTRATIONS—$1.00.

A work of unique interest, it being the only volume upon the subject. When one considers the marvelous changes in our fruits, vegetables and flowers within a generation, through the work of man in turning to his purposes the impulses of nature, the great interest of this may be indicated. It tells how varieties of cultivated plants come about, and further, how one may engage in the fascinating work of originating them.

## THE FORCING BOOK.

A manual of th cultivation of vegetables in glass hous s By L. H. Bailey, Professor of Horticulture in the Cornell University.

280 PAGES—38 ILLUSTRATIONS—$1 00.

No subject in horticulture has more rapidly assumed importance than that of bringing into use, out of season, various vegetables and fruits. If one stops to think of the deprivation there would be, even of the danger to health, n the cessation of this "forcing," and further, if an idea is gained of the extensive business done in out-of-season products,the importance of this complete little manual will be understood. It describes the best forcing-houses; tells what crops may be grown and marketed, and how best to do the work.

## THE PRUNING BOOK.

A monograph of the pruning and training of plants as a plied to the America c nditions. By L H. Bailey, Pr fes r of Hoit. culture in the Cornell University.

540 PAGES—332 ILLUSTRATIONS—$1.50.

Until the appearance of this book, there had been no complete and con-isi ent discussion of pruning. Professor Bailey considers fully the philosophy of the subject, showing why we should prune, with such statements of experience and observati n as will enlighten the reader It states principles: and then the various practices of prun ng are considered in full detail, and a vast fund of carefully collected data is made serviceable to the reader. The illustrations are remarkably fine.

## GARDEN MAKING.

Suggestions for the utilizing of home grounds. By L.H. Bailey, assisted by L. R. Taft, F. A. Waugh, and Ernest Wa ker.

417 PAGES—256 ILLUSTRATIONS—$1.00.

Here is a book, literally "for the million" who in Broad America have some love for growing things "Every family can have a garden. Wherever there is sunlight pl nts may be made to grow: and one plant in a tin can may be a more helpful and inspiring garden to some mind than a whole acre of lawn and flowers may be to another." The book is one to instruct, inspire and educate the reader. It tells of ornamental gardening of any range, treats of fruits and of vegetables for home use, and is useful alike to the owner of a suburban garden plot and the owner of a "little place" in the country. No modern American work covers this important field. The illustrations are copious and beautiful.

## LESSONS WITH PLANTS.

Suggestions for seeing and interpreting some of the common forms of vegetation. By L. H. Bailey, Professor of Horticulture in the Cornell University.

491 PAGES—446 ILLUSTRATIONS—HALF LEATHER 12MO—$1.10.

Profusely illustrated with delineations from nature, by W. S. Holdsworth, assistant Professor of Drawing in the Agricultural College of Michigan, carefully chosen and well executed. An extension of the ideas embodied in the "nature study leaflets," a part of the instruction given in the itinerant schools of horticulture in New York state.

## FIRST LESSONS WITH PLANTS

The first twenty chapters of the larger work described above.

117 PAGES—116 ILLUSTRATIONS—CLOTH 12MO 40 CENTS.

All of the illustrations of the original appear in these selected chapters which are in no way abbreviated.

"A remarkably well printed and well illustrated book, extremely original and unusually practical."—H. W. Foster, Ithaca, N. Y.

## THE SURVIVAL OF THE UNLIKE.

A collection of evolution essays suggested by the study of Domestic plants. By L. H. Bailey, Professor of Horticulture in the Cornell University.

SECOND EDITION—515 PAGES—22 ILLUSTRATIONS $2.00.

To those interested in the underlying philosophy of plant life, this volume, written in a most entertaining style, and fully illustrated, will prove welcome. It treats of the modification of plants under cultivation upon the evolution theories, and its attitude is characterized by the author's well known originality and independence of thought. Incidentally there is stated much that is valuable and suggestive to the working horticulturist. It may well be called, indeed, a philosophy of horticulture.

## THE EVOLUTION OF OUR NATIVE FRUITS.

By L. H. Bailey, Professor of Horticulture in the Cornell University.

485 PAGES—125 ILLUSTRATIONS—$2 00.

In this entertaining volume, the origin and developement of the fruits peculiar to North America are inquired into, and the personality of those horticultural pioneers whose almost forgotten labors have given us our most valuable fruits is touched upon. Th re has been careful research into the history of the various fruits, including inspection of the records of great European botani-ts who have given attention to American economic botany. The conclusions reached,the information presented and the suggestions as to future developments cannot but be valuable to any thoughtful fruit-grower, while the terse style of the author is at its best in his treatment of the subject.

## THE PRINCIPLES OF AGRICULTURE.

A text book for schools and rural societies. Edited by L. H. Bailey, with contributions from his colleagues in the Cornell University.

300 PAGES—92 ILLUSTRATIONS—$1.25

This is an attempt to analyze the complex subject of agriculture, and to present the underlying principles and factors in clear, terse English. Each chapter is in two parts: the first part, or the principles, i in numbered paragraphs in very large type (the size used in "Lessons with Plants"); the second part contains informal suggestions to the teacher and pupil, with illustrations. It is one of the few attempts to co-ordinate all the various agricultural subjects, showing the relative importance and position of each. It is a skeleton of agricultural science and practice. Full references are made to available literature.

We will send these books postpaid to any address on receipt of price.

# L. J. FARMER,

## PULASKI, N. Y.

# "PLANET JR." GARDEN TOOLS.

☞ Space will not permit illustrating and describing all of the Planet Jr. tools, but we will gladly send a full illustrated catalogue to any one who desires it; and we can supply promptly anything ordered. Planet Jr goods are standard machines, the best on the market. In sending your order to us you can rely on getting bottom prices.

---

### Planet Jr. Double Wheel Hoe.

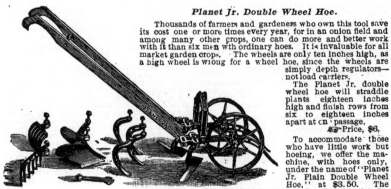

Thousands of farmers and gardeners who own this tool save its cost one or more times every year, for in an onion field and among many other crops, one can do more and better work with it than six men with ordinary hoes. It is invaluable for all market garden crops. The wheels are only ten inches high, as a high wheel is wrong for a wheel hoe, since the wheels are simply depth regulators—not load carriers.

The Planet Jr. double wheel hoe will straddle plants eighteen inches high and finish rows from six to eighteen inches apart at one passage. ☞Price, $6,

To accommodate those who have little work but hoeing, we offer the machine, with hoes only, under the name of "Planet Jr. Plain Double Wheel Hoe," at $3.50. The other parts can be added at any time and will be found to fit.

---

### The Planet Jr. No. 8 Horse Hoe.

Probably no other cultivating machine is so widely known as the Planet Jr. combined horse hoe and cultivator, for it is used throughout the civilized world. It is so strongly built as to withstand incredible strain, yet it is light and easy to handle. Every part is perfected to make the tool acceptable to the intelligent farmer who knows the best is always the cheapest. ☞Price, $8. Without depth regulator, $7.50.

---

### THE PLANET JR. NO. 5 HORSE HOE.

This tool is similar to the number eight horse hoe, but it has a plain wheel instead of one operated by a convenient lever.

☞Price, $6 75

---

### The Planet Jr. 12-Tooth Strawberry Cultivator and Harrow.

This comparatively new tool has rapidly grown into favor with market gardeners and strawberry growers. It is carefully made and finished, has a high frame and the chisel-shaped teeth cut an inch wide each, and may be worn down three inches before that width is lessened or the teeth worn out; even then they are cheaply replaced. It may be set with teeth trailing by simply changing one bolt in each tooth. The foot lever pulverizer is a capital addition for preparing ground for the seed drill or for plant setting. Hand levers regulate both width and depth while in motion; it can be contracted to 12 inches, and may be further reduced in width by taking off the outside teeth; it expands to 32 inches. It cultivates deep without throwing earth upon the plant, and the smooth, round throated teeth turn strawberry runners without injuring them. ☞Price, plain, $5.40; with wheel, $6.65; complete, $8.

# EXPRESS OR FREIGHT ORDER SHEET.

Parties in ordering, will oblige us by using this sheet, being careful to fill the spaces correctly. Before writing the order, please see advice on ordering. See other side for mail order sheet.

## L. J. FARMER, Pulaski, N. Y.

Name ........................................  P. O. Order, $...........

Post Office ..................................  Draft,  - -  ...........

County ......................................  Cash,   - -  ...........

State .......................................  Total, $.........

Express Office.................  Freight Station...................

Express Co.....................  Railroad ..........................

| Quantity. | Names of Plants Ordered. | Size or Age. | Price. |
|-----------|--------------------------|--------------|--------|
|  |  |  |  |
|  |  |  |  |
|  |  |  |  |
|  |  |  |  |
|  |  |  |  |
|  |  |  |  |
|  |  |  |  |
|  |  |  |  |
|  |  |  |  |
|  |  |  |  |
|  |  |  |  |
|  |  |  |  |
|  |  |  |  |
|  |  |  |  |
|  |  |  |  |
|  |  |  |  |
|  |  |  |  |
|  |  |  |  |
|  |  |  |  |

See Other Side for Mail Order Sheet.

We pack everything and deliver to freight, express and postoffice FREE. Patrons will accommodate us by clubbing with neighbors and making their orders as large as possible. The expense of filling a small order is often as great as a large one. Farmer's Fruit Farmer FREE with orders amounting to $1.00 or more.

# MAIL ORDER SHEET.

**L. J. FARMER, Pulaski, N. Y.** —Please send by mail to address given below.

Name........................................    P. O. Order, $ ........ ....

Post Office...................................    Stamps,   -      ............

County......................................    Cash,   -  -    ............

State............................................    Total, $............

*See Other Side for Express or Freight Order Sheet.*

| Quantity. | Name of Plants Ordered. | Price. |
|---|---|---|
| .......... | ........................................ | ...... .. |
| .......... | ........................................ | ........ |
| .......... | ........................................ | ........ |
| .......... | ........................................ | ........ |
| .......... | ........................................ | ........ |
| .......... | ........................................ | ........ |
| .......... | ........................................ | ........ |
| .......... | ........................................ | ........ |
| .......... | ........................................ | ........ |
| .......... | ........................................ | ........ |
| .......... | ........................................ | ........ |
| .......... | ........................................ | ........ |
| .......... | ........................................ | ........ |
| .......... | ........................................ | ........ |
| .......... | ........................................ | ........ |
| .......... | ........................................ | ........ |
| .......... | ........................................ | ........ |
| .......... | ........................................ | ........ |
| .......... | ........................................ | ........ |
| .......... | ........................................ | ........ |

**Be sure to add 20 cents postage per hundred on Strawberries, and 50 cents per hundred on Raspberries, Blackberries, Grapes, etc...** ... *L. J. FARMER.*

# PERSONAL TO YOU

Pulaski, N. Y., February 15, 1899.

Dear Friend:—Will you, this year, make an especial effort in our behalf? We need your help. The rich and old established firms who have plenty of money to invest in colored plates and expensive catalogues, can do without your trade. We cannot and live. Our prices are just. We do not ask the fancy rates of city firms who have to buy their plants of others; neither do we advertise a few varieties at ruinously low prices, expecting to make up on other items. Our prices are regulated by the supply. New varieties being necessarily higher.

We ask you to do all you can towards securing subscribers for Farmer's Fruit Farmer. Like our Nursery, it is not a large affair; but we hope to make everything in it readable. Many papers are not half read. We offer liberal terms to canvassers and club agents. Try and do something for us among your neighbors, in your Grange or Farmers' Club.

Yours for fruits,

L. J. FARMER.

---

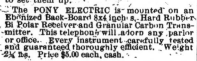

# CASH PRICE LIST

— OF —

# SPRAY PUMPS AND NOZZLES,

Manufactured by

## THE DEMING COMPANY,

### SALEM, OHIO.

THE LOW PRICES in this circular are given to introduce the "World's Best" Sprayers in your section. Perhaps one or more of your neighbors would club in with you and thus save freight.

When ready to order, if you find our Sprayers on sale in your town, we prefer that you give your order to our agent or dealer handling them. The prices herein are STRICTLY CONFIDENTIAL and are given for ONE INTRODUCTORY ORDER ONLY.

REMEMBER, that a copy of "Spraying for Profit," by Howard Evarts Weed, Entomologist, a highly illustrated treatise on insects and fungi destructive to plant life, and methods for their extermination, published price 20 cents, will be sent with each Sprayer ordered direct from us; and also,

Don't forget that if you want first to read the book, you can send us 20 cents in coin or stamps and we will send the book with a rebate certificate, which is good for 20 cents *when returned with the cash* amounting to the price of goods, less 20 cents.

We should be glad to receive from you a few addresses of parties interested in Horticulture.

## DIRECTIONS FOR ORDERING.

Write your order plainly on blank below; tear off this leaf at the perforation and mail with remittance, in envelope addressed to The Deming Company, Salem, Ohio.

Terms, cash with order. Delivered on board cars at any Railroad Depot or Express Office in Salem, Ohio.

How to send money. Send money by New York Draft, Postal Money Order, Express Money Order or Registered Letter.

Net Cash Prices are on next page, which is a part of this sheet. When torn off at the perforation it forms an Order Blank which must be returned to us, accompanied by the money; this insures accurate execution of your order.

## ORDER BLANK.—Goods specified on other side.

*THE DEMING CO., Salem, Ohio.* Date,........................................189....

*Dear Sirs:—Enclosed find.............................for which send by....................*
*(state if Express or Freight) articles marked on next page, at introductory cash prices of Sprayers, etc.*

Name...................................................................... Occupation.............................

Town............................................... County.......................... State......................

Remarks ...............................................................................................................

# SPECIAL CASH PRICES.

### Mark the goods ordered and carry out, adding the prices.

| Quantity Ordered. | FIGURE AND DESCRIPTION OF ARTICLES REPRESENTED BY ILLUSTRATIONS ON FOLLOWING PAGES. | Net Cash Prices | Carry Out and Add |
|---|---|---|---|
| .......... | Fig. 689, "Perfect Success" Brass Spray Pump (patent) for Bucket. Pump clamps to bucket and bail is held upright........................ | $ 4.00 | .......... |
| .......... | 7-ft. section of hose and pole connection for same for tree spraying........... | 1.00 | .......... |
| .......... | Fig. 675, "Success" Knapsack Sprayer with copper tank and Brass Pump; extra handle for use like Bucket Pump........................ | 9.50 | .......... |
| .......... | 7-ft. section of hose and pole connection for same for tree spraying........... | 1.00 | .......... |
| .......... | Fig. 651, Gardener's Choice Spray Cart with Gem Pump........................ | 9.50 | .......... |
| .......... | 7-ft. section of hose and pole connection for tree spraying........................ | 1.00 | .......... |
| .......... | Fig. 550, Deming Brass-lined Barrel Sprayer with Automatic Agitator Pump only, with 3-way discharge cocks for hose........................ | 5.00 | .......... |
| .......... | Fig. 550, Outfit A, same as above, with 12½-ft. section of ½-inch hose, couplings, pole connection and Bordeaux Nozzle. | 7.50 | .......... |
| .......... | Fig. 550, Outfit B, same as above, with two 12½-ft. sections of ½-inch hose, nozzle, etc........................ | 10.00 | .......... |
| .......... | Fig. 653, The Deming 4-row Field Sprayer for Potatoes, Tobacco, Cotton, Plants, etc. Attachable to any Wagon and Barrel Sprayer; adjustable to tall or short plants; forward or backward spray, and rows 30 to 40 inches apart. Everything controlled from the wagon........................ | 7.50 | .......... |
| .......... | Fig. 649, "Success" Kerosene Sprayer (patent). Mixes automatically oil and water in desired proportions, controlled by an indicator gauge. A great labor saver, dispensing with making Kerosene Emulsion........................ | 7.00 | .......... |
| .......... | 7-ft. section of hose and pole connection for same for tree spraying........ | 1.00 | .......... |
| .......... | Fig. 529, Peerless Barrel Kerosene Sprayer Pump (patent), with Brass working parts, tank of copper, Agitator, etc., without hose; has 3-way discharge cock. Kerosene tank and attachments can be taken off and agitator connected for ordinary spraying—a great machine........................ | 14.00 | .......... |
| .......... | Fig. 529, Outfit A, same as above, with 12½-ft. section of ½-inch hose and pole connection, couplings and Bordeaux Nozzle........................ | 16.50 | .......... |
| .......... | Fig. 529, Outfit B, same as above, with two 12½-ft. sections of hose and pole connections, etc........................ | 19.00 | .......... |
| | (Above prices of Fig. 529 and outfits for Iron Air Chamber; with Brass Air Chamber, $2.50 net, extra.) | | |
| .......... | Fig. 676, Weed Knapsack Kerosene Sprayer (patent). The oil tank, like in Fig. 649, can be detached for using in regular way........................ | 13.50 | .......... |
| .......... | Fig. 965, Bordeaux Patent Spray Nozzles. Solid stream graduated to coarse or fine, or long distance for trees; easily degorged. World's Best. | 65 | .......... |
| .......... | Fig. 963, Deming-Vermorel Patent Spray Nozzle, makes a mist-like spray, a great improvement over the old style Vermorel Nozzle........................ | 65 | .......... |
| .......... | Fig. 749, hose stock for connecting to spray nozzles........... | 15 | .......... |
| .......... | Fig. 966, Combination Coupling for connecting our Spray Nozzles to ¼ or ¾-in. hose coupling........................ | 15 | .......... |
| .......... | Fig. 971, Extension Pole, brass connection........................ | 40 | .......... |
| .......... | Fig. 980, Brass Double Spraying Attachment, with pole connection........ | 60 | .......... |
| .......... | Fig. 955, Sherman Patent Hose Band for ½-in. hose, each........................ | 06 | .......... |
| .......... | Fig. 949, Brass Hose Couplings for ½-in. hose, as used on Barrel Sprayers. Per pair, as per cut........................ | 12 | .......... |
| .......... | Fig. 949, Brass Hose Couplings for ¾-in. hose or tubing, as used on Bucket and Knapsack Sprayers........................ | 10 | .......... |
| .......... | Rubber Hose for Barrel Sprayers, ½-in., per foot........................ | 10 | .......... |
| .......... | Rubber Tubing for Bucket and Knapsack Sprayers, per foot........... | 08 | .......... |
| | IF ORDER AMOUNTS TO $25.00 or over, deduct 5 per cent. from this (gross total) footing........................ | | |
| | This Amount of Cash (NET TOTAL) enclosed with order........................ | | |

*If this column in your order foots over $25.00, we will allow 5 per cent. discount.*

DIRECTIONS FOR ORDERING on other side (first page). The order must be written on this sheet, which may be detached. Write shipping directions plainly on other side.

# SPRAYERS, NOZZLES AND APPLIANCES.
## THE DEMING CO., Salem, Ohio.
The order blank containing descriptions and prices is detachable from this sheet.

Fig. 689.  Fig. 675.  Fig. 651.

Fig. 653.

Fig. 550.

## "Has Given Unqualified Satisfaction."

THE DEMING COMPANY, Salem, Ohio.  SHIOCTON, WIS., Dec. 7, 1897.
Dear Sirs:—I am still using the "Success" Pump and Bordeaux Nozzle which I got of you two years ago. It has given unqualified satisfaction. Nothing has ever been out of order about it, and it has never failed to meet all demands made on it. I still think, as I did then, that it is the best thing of its kind on the market, and that no florist—amateur or commercial —can afford to get along without one.  Yours very truly,  EBEN E. REXFORD,
*Floricultural Editor "Ladies' Home Journal."*

We have hundreds of testimonials as unqualified as the above.

RESPONSIBILITY.—We have the best equipped Pump factory in the world, and make the largest line of Hand, Wind-Mill and Power Pumps. We refer to Farmers' Nat'l and First Nat'l Banks, and to Adams' and Wells-Fargo Express Agents in our city, also to any of the State Agricultural Experiment Stations, nearly all of which use our sprayers or nozzles.

# SPRAYERS, NOZZLES AND APPLIANCES.

## THE DEMING CO., Salem, Ohio.

The order blank containing descriptions and prices is detachable from this sheet.

Fig. 649.　　　　Fig. 529.

Fig. 676.

Fig. 971.

Fig. 980.　Fig. 955.

Fig. 965.　Fig. 963.　Fig. 749.　Fig. 966.　Fig. 949.

No space for more testimonials on this page. This is a good one, however.

**"DOES SATISFACTORY WORK IN EVERY WAY."**

THE DEMING CO., Salem, Ohio.　　　　FORT VALLEY, GA., Oct. 25th, 1898.

*Dear Sirs.*—During the past year I have had your **Peerless Kerosene Sprayer, Fig. 529,** in use on the various fruit farms of which I am manager. I find that the Sprayer *does satisfactory work in every way,* and while adapted for the use of Bordeaux Mixture or other fungicides and insecticides, yet it is particularly useful for the application of kerosene mechanically mixed with water for the destruction of scale insects and plant-lice. There are many scale insects, not as injurious as the San Jose scale, but it is about as essential to spray for these insects as it is to cultivate the trees, as it not only destroys these scale insects, but places the trees in a healthy condition, less liable to the attack of the more dangerous scales. The introduction of the mechanical mixture of kerosene and water, by means of your kerosene sprayers, however, makes a simple and effective remedy for the suppression of the scale. I feel certain that everyone interested in fruit growing, even for home use, would purchase one of these sprayers if they knew their value.　　　Yours truly,　　　C. W. WITHOFT,
　　　Manager of the Albaugh-Georgia Fruit Co. and the Ohio Fruit Land Co., etc., Fort Valley, Georgia, the most extensive fruit interests in the South.